Cursed to be a Fixer

Nikki Marie

Copyright © 2018 by Nikki Marie
All rights reserved. This book or any portion thereof
may not be reproduced or used in any manner whatsoever
without the express written permission of the publisher
except for the use of brief quotations in a book review.
Printed in the United States of America

First Printing, 2018

ISBN 978-0578407661

Honey520
San Antonio, TX

www.Honey520.co

"Imagine me with knives in my back but I'm trying to heal you"

Cover Illustration: Cease Martinez

Words Heal

Prelude

What inspires you to wake up each day? For me, if at least one reader can relate and somehow find a drop of inspiration then this journey is completely worth it for me. My motivation comes from a special boy named Noah who makes life worth living. I'm a Latina, writer, hairstylist, makeup artist, mother, daughter, sister, advocate, and I am still learning.

I'm an old soul who's had her share of pain and brokenness on a road to self worth hoping each reader finds theirs. So enclosed is my naked soul expressing myself in my purest form ….

Fixers

Some people on this earth love so genuinely and they are as raw as honey. Those kinds of people are the ones that lookout for you and worry about you when you're not at your best. They may have had a troubled past or did not grow up in the most favorable conditions and yet they still love so hard. These fixers attract others in need of healing because they know what it feels like to be broken. They know what it feels like to be abandoned when they needed somebody to be there and know how it feels to need support only to not get it in return. Most of all they know what it feels like to feel like they aren't enough. Fixers want to nurture others back to health and no one tells you about the side effects from being this nurturing person. This person gives and gives whether it's to one person or several people. After a while this person is running on empty because what they give is rarely reciprocated. They choose to surround themselves with others that are a reflection of their past or what they think they deserve. They tend to run with the little bit they receive to refuel them but it's never enough so they continue to try to fix. If I'm describing you then it is time to make a change. The hardest work is self work because it takes a level of honesty and vulnerability to understand you. It is time to unlearn and detox what isn't serving you. Most of all it is time to love what is serving you. You deserve loyalty, respect, and you're capable of receiving genuine healthy love. You have always been enough. If you have one of these rare gems in your life, appreciate them because in this cold world not everyone will love like that.

Caged

Absolutely no freedom with your mind
Emotions caged unable to fly
Always having to consider someone else's feelings
Freedom is never completely free
It's costs a level of authenticity and disconnection
It costs transparency in a world full of lies
Everything has a price even to fly

***To understand we must start from the beginning
it's time to open the cage***

Forgiveness is for me

Robbed of my innocence
The pureness of my mentality just ripped away
Hoping this would eventually fade away like a distant memory
Hoping what was in front of me wasn't real
Nothing but fear and anger is what I feel
Why didn't I scream?
Why didn't I hit you?
Why did I freeze?
Questions I can't answer looking in the mirror
I can't forgive him but worse I can't forgive myself
For the girl who wasn't strong enough
If I can go back…
I would hold her and tell her she's going to be okay
I would tell her not to be afraid
It's a ghost that still haunts for years to come
It's a door that welcomed abuse that's finally shut decades later
It's a woman who will always feel a little numb
It's someone who just wants to be protected but loved
It's a woman who finally knows healing
Robbed and Courageous

Anxiety

The overwhelming feeling of no control over all the things
that tear you down
All the nervousness comes in because you don't know what
to do
You tremble and shake
Wondering if maybe there's something you can maybe take
To make all of it go away
Or maybe you just need to disappear
And let go of all the fears
Tears keep coming down your face
You want to scream while crying
All you feel is your heart pounding fast pace
When will I come down from this unbearable anxiety

Just breathe

Devoted and Naive

When I met you I had fire for you
It burned bright
your charm and confidence were contagious
No judgements or explanations
I knew I wanted to be yours
No faults or expectations

Then it happened
The first disappointment and the doubts started to surface
our happiness was tainted
Flaws appeared that resurfaced the doubts

but I still stayed
I believed in change
you still have something to prove to the old you
and I believed in you
there was no giving up

-Cursed to be a fixer

The lesson

The basic needs in a relationship are never a grand gesture
We live in a generation that values all the things that don't bear fruit
As if being faithful is something that's a gift given but should be as basic as the water you need
When you starve me of my needs all you're teaching me is how to live without your supply and how to live without you
You're teaching me how to adjust and fly on my own

You're teaching me strength I never knew I wanted
you're teaching me that you're not the picture I painted you to be
The picture is just art on a wall

And that is the lesson you're teaching me

Why I hate your phone

There's a reason why I cringe when you have your phone in your hands and why I feel sick when you smile at it. Maybe because it pulls you in as I am trying to reach out.
I hate when I found the courage to look at everything in it, I lost my confidence.
I hate that it is filled with messages and pictures that caught your interest.
I hate that it's just a reminder of how my pictures aren't in there. A reminder that no memory was important enough for you to capture and no picture of me was delightful enough to look at for you to save.

The secrets seem to pile up in there as well as the private conversations you give attention to.
Your phone is a constant reminder of how I'm not important enough in your world away from me.
Not important enough to leave a mark in your device.
It's a reminder how the inconsiderate nature you possess does not allow you to communicate when you're out.
I hate your phone because each time it goes off I lose a piece of myself but most of all I lose peace.

I'm worth more than your phone

Poison

I'm barely surviving on a tiny dose of trust for you
The past is like poison that spreads in my veins and it infects every inch of me
Living with thoughts of him with someone else
Wondering if his mind travels far from me maybe underneath her clothes
Asking myself if I'll ever be enough to quench that enormous thirst he holds
My mind is at war, my heart is still bleeding, and my soul has no peace
This poison is making me ill

I can wonder where he's at and I can wonder who he's with but what remains is the condition of his heart

This poison infects peace

Matters of the heart

Your doubts grow vines and they spread quickly
You replay everything they ever said over and over again
Second guessing facts and so called truths
Your intuition screaming for your heart to listen
Maybe if the heart listens it can be spared this time
The brain wants to take over to stay logical but your heart
knows you're not being fair
Then you feel it drop so far from your chest when truth
comes knocking on your door just to confirm intuition
The heart has no choice but to hear truth

The heart never gets spared

To her better known as the side chick

You think you have the upper hand in the situation because you know about me.
You think you got him in a place I don't because he didn't tell me about you. You think you're better than me thinking I can't fulfill his needs. You think somewhere in that heart of his that you are inside it. You think you're loyal because you keep his secret. You think you can keep your fantasy alive if you keep the intimacy with him and that he'll make you his one day. You watch my every move thinking I'm a fool and wonder if my female intuition has revealed any assumption about you. You look at my pictures and compare me to you.
You really think you've won the battle
You think…
But you've lost the war within yourself.

I am a woman flawed and all but carry myself with integrity. It took me a long time to love myself after a chapter of abuse and heartache. That love for me is so deeply rooted and my worth can't be tainted. The issue of him not being faithful lies within himself. As he fights his own demons let me remind you that it's nothing I'm lacking as a woman. Every relationship has ups and downs and there will always be temptation. As he slips away into it, there will always be a woman that will seek affection where she can find it. As angry as I should be, I mostly feel sadness. Sadness that you don't love yourself enough to think you deserve more. Sadness that you think being intimate with a man who's spoken for that you will have something to gain. Sadness that you never felt like you were worth enough. Become the person you were meant to love.

I pray you find healing....

Sincerely,
The woman who knows we both deserve better

Irony

We treat the people that care about us poorly whether it is family, close friends, or our significant other. We take them for granted and pay more attention to their flaws than any good they do. We don't support them like we should or take the time to celebrate their personal victories. We should be their biggest fans but yet we give all that to people who wouldn't put in that kind of care or work for us....

Appreciate what you have before it becomes what you had

Healing doesn't live here

I find no peace no matter where I search for it
Your offense pierces my thoughts with the sharpest sword there is
You live in my heart but the wound can't live here anymore
How can I have one without the other when they are hand in hand
Healing won't come when my wound won't stop bleeding
Healing seems so far away because I haven't imagined tomorrow without you yet

One has to go

Somebody's daughter

Every argument and every unloving word spoken is another cut on me
Every grain of salt thrown by you to my wounds is a reminder of what resides inside of you
Everything a father would despise about a man who would treat their daughter in such a manner is everything you are

I am somebody's daughter too
Don't forget

Sweeter than your solitude

I know being a part of my life wasn't planned or easy.
I see your look of good intent
I see pain that you hide from old disappointments
I see the desire for a better life
I see the desire to be a better man

I don't want to be the woman you're just passing time with
I never felt so far from you but yet I'm next to you
I long to be sweeter than your solitude

Still Hopeful

Empathy

I try to understand why your pride won't let you love
You feel like you're losing control if you start to feel
Showing you care is a form of weakness for you
When I cried my eyes to sleep while you slept soundly next to me
is when I knew you had no empathy

Love doesn't reside in you

They mattered

Those sweet good morning messages mattered
Those messages during the day to say you're thinking about me mattered
Those compliments you would freely give always mattered
Your display of affection for me made me feel special
It's not just about the way you made me feel when you stopped but how can I elevate you when I feel completely defeated?

The little things always mattered

Your corner

I was always for you not against you
I was reaching when you weren't reaching
You're a man with a past for a purpose
The past was not your home when I was your present
I wish you can take my eyes and look in the mirror then you might see
Maybe one day you will

I was always for you but not for me

The fixer

Always trying to fix someone else's problems
Always trying to make somebody feel better
Always trying to heal someone's damaged roots that trace back decades ago
Always trying to glue broken pieces that aren't yours to glue
Always trying to take the sharp scissors away and save someone from themselves

Who's gluing your shattered pieces together
Who's saving your soul
Who's giving you peace
Who's healing your decades of generational bondage

The time is now
Time to save yourself
Time to save your generation

Self Awareness

Unapologetic

I apologize for having standards and high expectations
I apologize for elevating you if you were never going to live
up to it
I apologize for having responsibilities and for being cooped
up wanting you with me
I'm sorry for not being the woman out catching your eye or
the woman taking off her clothes
Most of all I apologize for my sharp sword of a tongue

Sorry I'm not sorry at all

Her shoes

Put yourself in my shoes for once. Imagine a person coming into your life showing you greatness and makes you believe in yourself again. This person comes in and charms their way into your heart. You start building a life and a possible future. You actually go against your better judgement and take no precautions. Everyone warns you of their past but you still want to love this once broken person. They hurt you give you every trust issue, and insecurity a person can possible feel. They grow cold and start becoming someone you don't recognize anymore but you're already so invested. You continue to give and give of yourself but nothing is reciprocated. You don't want to let it go because you're literally hanging on potential but you are drowning while this person is watching and doing nothing to save you. You find yourself hopeless in the memory of what was and when everything in your life is screaming at you to let it go you're still holding on to it for dear life swimming against the tides. You start remembering every rejection you've ever felt and you start wondering where in life did you stop loving yourself to accept this. Imagine being at home waiting for my call but I'm careless. Imagine trying to keep everything intact running on empty. Think of yourself lying awake in your darkest hours wondering why you're alone and wondering why you're not enough. Think of how it feels to keep trying to see empathy in someone who's so cold. Think of what it feels like having to hide the pain to make it through the day. Imagine loving someone so broken but you're broken yourself. Imagine me with knives in my back and one big one in my heart but trying to heal you. This is why I always end up hurt.

His shoes

You say put myself in your shoes, well put yourself in mine. Imagine having all your freedom and freewill away for close to a decade. Imagine having people stuck with you everyday for that decade having no space, no freedom, and no free will. Now imagine whenever you needed someone no one was there just you. Just think of how your whole damn mind and thought process can be altered because all you know is yourself. Think of being degraded day in and day out and think of being mind screwed and locked in a cage for this decade. Think of all the so called love ones nowhere to be found and you all alone think how you would deal with emotion when knowing all you have is you. Think of being at your lowest with no one but you and when you can imagine this, you could never feel how it feels to wish you were dead cause all you see is absurdity and death around you and no way to escape it cause you're stuck in the midst of it. Think how your mental state would be. Think of how it feels to be 100% emotionally numb cause all you've known for the past years is nobody gives a damn and all you have is you. This is why I don't do relationships.

Repercussions

I don't wake up crazy looking for faults
I wake up with this enemy called old memories
They are memories of letdowns
They are memories of past disappointments
They run through my thoughts and manifest in my actions
which stirs up attitudes and frustrations
Then you make a mistake that triggers a whole chapter full
of faults and the words roll right off my tongue and there it
is, the first disagreement of the day
Then you say I'm crazy as if your past actions have no
repercussions
I'm not crazy
I'm just a woman who struggles with forgiveness

And there we go

The flip

You have this way of downplaying every mistake you make
Yet you have a magnifying glass on me
When I bring up a problem it's my fault for bringing up the problem
You have this way of flipping every situation to cater to your negative attributes so you don't have to be wrong
And I can just look like the one of the crazy women in your past sitting on your shelf collecting dust that you display just to prove that we are all at fault.

Add me to the collection

Social Media

Don't you know I'm always going to be one step ahead?
I'm always going to know the details about your life that you won't give
I'm going to know about your ex and all the girls you were interested in
I'm going to know your type and all the things that you admire
I'm going to see every like and comment you display
Don't you know I'm going to know way more than I let on?
Don't you know I can find out anything about anything?

Never underestimate any curious woman

My needs

You shut me out
If I can't talk to you about life and our relationship then tell me who can I talk to?
Where do I go for comfort?
Where do I go for encouragement when I need it?
Who do I share my dreams with?
Don't starve me then ask me where I'm getting my nutrients from

Communication

Princess Syndrome

He says I have princess syndrome because I don't settle
Because I know what I'm willing to give so I expect nothing less from him
Because I won't be mistreated or played with like a toy
For I have a mind of my own that needs stimulation
I'm have my own thoughts and opinions that differ from his so I won't be mute
I know what I bring to the table and I know how to decorate it with my sweet touch that you can't find anywhere else
If your maximum is my bare minimum then yes I must confess I have princess syndrome because chivalry is not dead for this princess

Not entitled just worth it

King of Mixed Signals

I feel like I am almost forcing you to be mine and you resent me for it. I feel like all the things that should come natural I've had to ask for them. You keep saying things will be different but I don't know who is more at fault. Is it me for not accepting what is or you for fooling me? I have always felt more invested in this relationship than you. You showed you cared in the beginning and only when I'm walking away. The bottom line is we all put in effort and make time for the things we care about. I just don't feel like I'm one of them anymore so why do you not cut me loose?

> I know I am flawed but you've never had to question whether I care about you or where my heart lies.

You left the revolving door open again

Ropes upon Ropes

Undo this attachment
Untangle this knot we formed
Don't pull this rope in after I loosen it
I don't trust what you'll pull me into

Today I wear black to grieve you

I need to wake up and feel okay
I need to not miss your presence
I need to feel whole again without you
So today I say goodbye to all the fear
I say goodbye to the insecurities
I say goodbye to everything I knew with you
Today is the day I grieve you
And tomorrow I move on without you
I remember the woman I was before
She was whole by herself
She was brave
She was fierce
She was fire
I need to find her and not let her go
She was going places

I won't forget her again
Letting go of you and remembering me

Day 1

It feels so lonely today
No one to be mad at
Everything replays from the last disagreement
I was going to text you good morning but I stopped myself
Hours passed and the evening came
I was going to ask if we can take back our last words but I stopped myself
Before I went to bed I wanted to call to hear your voice
My pride saved me
I have a village behind me for support but they are not you holding me close at night
And this is just day 1

Day by day I will be okay

The Art of Letting Go

You said you would change,
I don't want to miss that
I can't see you with anyone else or changed for someone new
I deserve the effort
I invested too much
I miss the routine
I miss you

I had no choice and I had to let it go but I didn't want to bleed

But it rushed out of me like the tears did when no one was around
You weren't there when I cried my eyes to sleep replaying everything
You didn't reach out for me when I craved your touch
You didn't feel my pain wondering why I wasn't enough
You didn't read the messages in draft that never got sent
Or how every bit of peace was gone wondering what you might be doing
My resentment grew thinking about the pain
Being bitter just made it easier to not want you anymore

The bleeding stopped and healing started like a dry scab

You'll never know how long it took just to feel okay

I didn't want to be bitter anymore
So I was fixing me
Time was passing
I started to fall in love with what I was fixing
I caught myself starting to smile
I was enjoying life again
I remembered who I was before you
I was thanking you for that lesson
I was finally letting go

It is better for the wound to bleed out and heal than to be cut often just to re open the wound. There's no healing in staying and when you are free, the scars will be beautiful.

The Attraction

You were taught not to show weakness
I was taught humility
You were taught not to break
I was shown how to cry
You had to learn survival
I was a natural nurturer
You were broken
I wanted to fix
How can the attraction be questioned?

Familiar spirits

Mirrors

What do you do when you look in the mirror and you see a face you don't recognize?
You see dark circles of many sleepless nights
You see puffy eyes from the many nights of crying yourself to sleep
You see fine lines where you've never seen them before from stress
That's when you realize you haven't taken care of yourself like you should have
You see the happiness has diminished off of you somewhere
I don't recognize this woman looking back at me
I don't like mirrors anymore
She's not free
She's not the girl I remember
She's not vibrant anymore
I must find her and pull her out of this dark place
I must rid of her demons

I need familiar

Just so you know

Our last night together I was growing weary of us
I had nothing left of me to give
I felt so drained thinking of the all the times I tried to make you see you were losing me
Our last disagreement was like a ticking time bomb we both expected
I cried my eyes to sleep not because you hurt my feelings again but because that was going to be the last time
I wasn't crying because I'm sensitive
I was crying because I knew I had to mourn us

Just so you know I knew I had to let you go

The tree

My thoughts seem to travel to a place I never want to leave. A place of comfort but confusion clouds my reality. He shows me how I am to be treated and understands a woman's worth. His loyalty is rooted like a thousand year old tree. The tree doesn't break or crumble at the sound of a loud thunderstorm but keeps a still peace. Am I to cave in and break under pressure? Do I confess what I know under my bones? Or am I stay in familiar waters that keep drowning me but at float when convenient? The waters I know can be rough and all consuming at times but the sound of the waves is music to my ears. But wait don't abandon that tree in your thoughts because someone else will find it and admire the rare breed it is. You see the tree doesn't ever change or move to another spot because it's ideal, it remains.

My place

Another time

There's not a day that goes by that I don't think of what could have been
We could've had the world in our hands
We could've had it all
Your love isn't safe
Your waters aren't still and the risk is big
Your impulse is far too great
I long for peace and stability
Sometimes I daydream of different circumstances
Like a hurt animal when you're wounded you bite
Like a hurt animal when wounded I hide
While I daydream I'll be just another chapter in your book

Stability

Boomerang

These emotions are too deep to ignore
Wasting your time convincing me that we aren't right for each other
Maybe one day we'll get it right
We can fight it but you'll find your way back
You give me that unpredictable
I give you that stability
You can leave but you'll find your way back
You give me that spontaneous
I give you that consistency
You can try to let go but you'll find your way back

It always returns

My war

Forgive me or leave me he says
Well don't you know I'm torn with what I should do?
Confusion divides me into pieces clouding my thoughts
I want you to do right by me but I also want to do right by me
Can I have both and still have you?

Why couldn't you appreciate me the first time?
And that is my war

Brown eyed girl

Don't worry brown eyed girl your time will come for you to shine
You never felt like you were good enough because you didn't look like the girls on TV or that beautiful girl in your class
You felt forgotten because you didn't speak up for yourself and being smart just didn't come as easy
You didn't feel pretty in your lovely brown skin and because your hair wasn't silky smooth like the others
You never felt special because you came from a family that didn't have a lot of money
You never felt like you really fit in anywhere
All those characteristics you didn't like about yourself were making you unique
That naive little Girl will grow strong and speak her mind
That insecure little Girl will grow to love her wavy hair and will embrace her skin
That little girl will be so driven to achieve her dreams
That brown eyed girl will realize she was born to stand out

A note to my young self

Queens

You will never know all the weight I carry on my shoulders or all my battles but just know I'm fighting too. I just need me in my corner wiping the dirt off my face and straightening my crown...

Old Days are gone

You don't use your words vocally anymore
Since communication is only private messages, comments, likes, or text now
Which takes the place of any real interaction?
You don't need to compliment me anymore just press like on a picture
You don't need to ask about my day you can just leave a comment
You don't need to get to know me just do some research
You don't have to call you can just text

Let's take a tech break

The Dark Parts

I see the darkest parts of you and I still loved you
You see some of my flaws and you choose to magnify them
and destroy me
When did I love you more than you liked me?

My love is unconditional and yours had conditions

I represent you

I am an extension of you.
How you treat me is a reflection of how you see yourself
So why would anyone not want to value their partner when that's who you chose to represent you?

Food for thought

Changes

You want to see change then look in the mirror. You have a vision then work on it. You care for someone then show them. You love someone so tell them. It's time to turn goals into reality and show people there's humanity left. Tomorrow is a gift and is never promised.

Improving yourself so you can help others rise is the key to fulfillment

Suicide of potential

I've watched you kill every part of yourself that I fell in love with
You murdered that affectionate person that made me feel loved
I watched you drown yourself and go mute as you chose not to speak life into us anymore
That confident person choked on their insecurities and couldn't swallow their pride
Your ego grew and suffocated the humblest parts of you.
You're excitement for me faded like a failed heartbeat
May this person who had potential rest in peace with my expectations

RIP

Home

I dream of a love so authentic it sings to my soul a familiar song
Not a song I've heard before but a song that simply feels like home
A safe place where we flow so free in admiration
A love with endless growth
A place filled with compassion
It's a song that lifts my spirits
And sings of forgiveness
It's the freedom of being flawed and never abandoned
How do you know you found that love?
Because it feels like home.

Dear Mother,

You have become my inner voice when I don't feel adequate enough
I find myself always searching for your approval in everything I do
All I ever wanted was to make you proud even though it seems I never did
You were my biggest critic and I was so mad at you for that
I didn't understand you and all you held on to silently so we wouldn't be affected
I didn't see all the battles you fought alone

I was so hard on you
Then life gave me a pair of your shoes to wear
The fit was so uncomfortable and painful
The cycle came full circle
My heartache mirrored yours
For once I understood you
For the first time I remembered being a little girl looking at a woman who had to protect herself
I saw a woman who loved so hard
I saw the inheritance of strength

Dear Mother, I finally see you and I appreciate you

For My best friend

She says "I feel like he's really trying this time and I'm not ready to give up on him yet"
I look at all her beauty and see how talented she is
I don't understand how she thinks he is her equal.
I stand aside and watch this woman who should be treasured
Be with a man that doesn't deserve her.

I hope one day she finds a man that's equally yoked

Your mixed tape

I am like a classic mix tape
I am original and carefully mixed
I am that music you miss that isn't on your playlist anymore
I am that song you want to constantly replay because you didn't appreciate it the first time

Music to your ears

Standing Still

Standing still in a world moving so fast
Listening twice before you speak
Taking time to think before you react
Understanding before you judge

My feet are grounded

No Regrets

A heart breaking chapter in my book of life
I can only embrace the lesson
My tears were seen and my voice was heard
I remember the rough nights but I recall the warm ones too
Your love birthed a million poems out of me
I have no regrets
Now I can see reason through the ashes and I can find beauty in the chapter

The greatest peace

Unaffected

Stop and take in that moment when you're not thinking of that person anymore like you used to
You realize that missing them is old news
When thinking of them with some else doesn't make you sick anymore
Knowing they moved on doesn't affect you at all
Remembering the days when their name was in your search engine seems so distant now
All of that stress you used to feel is completely gone
All of that worry has eased itself out of your body
You look back and realize you survived a broken heart and those old memories don't linger around anymore
You understand time healed and you let go gracefully.

**You are officially unaffected*

Talking Walls

What would the walls say if they could talk?
Would they tell about the time I wasn't the victim
Would they recall that argument that went to far?
Would they speak about that rage I had from every bottled up emotion
Whose side would they take*?*

Your side, my side, or the truth that lies in between

No Longer Cursed but Blessed

You are Free
You are no longer cursed to fix
The only person that you must heal is you
Take care of that person in the mirror
You must see value so others will too
Self awareness is growth
Without growth is a spiritual death
You can always be better and you can always do more
Don't forget to live and enjoy this gift of life

My thoughts and poetry

If you are here, I thank you for reading my truth and the truth of others
Thank you for peaking into my soul and letting me be transparent
I pray each reader inspires somebody and helps others see their worth too

Change is coming

-Nikki Marie

Connect with Nikki Marie on social media
For news on her next book
And other exclusives

Instagram @nikkimarie520
Twitter @dearnikkimarie
Facebook @nikkimariebooks

www.ingramcontent.com/pod-product-compliance
Lightning Source LLC
Chambersburg PA
CBHW071416040426
42444CB00009B/2272